Contemporary Designs

STAINED GLASS
PATTERN BOOK

ANNA CROYLE

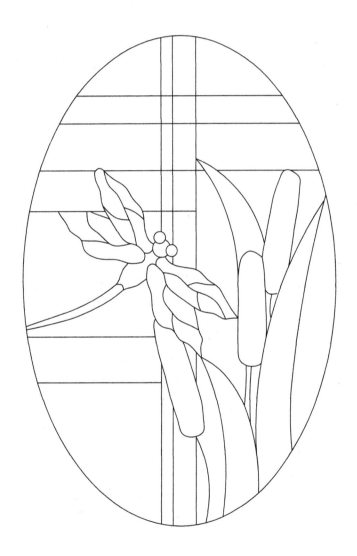

DOVER PUBLICATIONS, INC.
MINEOLA, NEW YORK

Planet Friendly Publishing
✔ Made in the United States
✔ Printed on Recycled Paper
Text: 30%   Cover: 10%
Learn more: www.greenedition.org

GREEN
EDITION

At Dover Publications we're committed to producing books in an earth-friendly manner and to helping our customers make greener choices.

Manufacturing books in the United States ensures compliance with strict environmental laws and eliminates the need for international freight shipping, a major contributor to global air pollution.

And printing on recycled paper helps minimize our consumption of trees, water and fossil fuels. The text of *Contemporary Designs Stained Glass Pattern Book* was printed on paper made with 30% post-consumer waste, the color insert was printed on paper made with 10% post-consumer waste, and the cover was printed on paper made with 10% post-consumer waste. According to Environmental Defense's Paper Calculator, by using this innovative paper instead of conventional papers, we achieved the following environmental benefits:

Trees Saved: 10 • Air Emissions Eliminated: 873 pounds
Water Saved: 3,915 gallons • Solid Waste Eliminated: 460 pounds

For more information on our environmental practices, please visit us online at www.doverpublications.com/green

Copyright

Bibliographical Note

Contemporary Designs Stained Glass Pattern Book is a new work, first published by Dover Publications, Inc., in 2009.

DOVER *Pictorial Archive* SERIES

This book belongs to the Dover Pictorial Archive Series. You may use the designs and illustrations for graphics and crafts applications, free and without special permission, provided that you include no more than four in the same publication or project. (For permission for additional use, please write to Permissions Department, Dover Publications, Inc., 31 East 2nd Street, Mineola, N.Y. 11501.)

However, republication or reproduction of any illustration by any other graphic service, whether it be in a book or in any other design resource, is strictly prohibited.

Library of Congress Cataloging-in-Publication Data

Croyle, Anna.
    Contemporary designs stained glass pattern book/ Anna Croyle.
       p. cm. — (Dover pictorial archive series)
    ISBN-13: 978-0-486-47176-1
    ISBN-10: 0-486-47176-4
    1. Glass craft—Patterns. 2. Glass painting and staining—Patterns. I. Title.
II. Title: Stained glass pattern book.

TT298.C757 2009
748.5—dc22
                                                          2009006509

Manufactured in the United States by Courier Corporation
47176401
www.doverpublications.com

NOTE

Cast a modern aura onto your next stained glass project with this wondrous treasury of contemporary designs. Featured here are a wide variety of precise and versatile black-and-white illustrations depicting flowers, insects, geometric configurations, and much more. The seventy patterns in this book may also be reproduced in larger or smaller sizes to best fit your individual stained glass project. A sixteen-page insert (located between pp. 28 and 29) displays each dynamic design in color.

This collection of patterns is intended as a supplement to stained glass instruction books (such as *Stained Glass Craft Made Simple* by James McDonell, Dover Publications, Inc., 0-486-24963-8). All materials needed, including general instructions and tools for beginners, can usually be purchased from local craft or hobby stores, or on the Internet.

Peonies

1

Loves Me, Loves Me Not

Bonnie's Gardenia

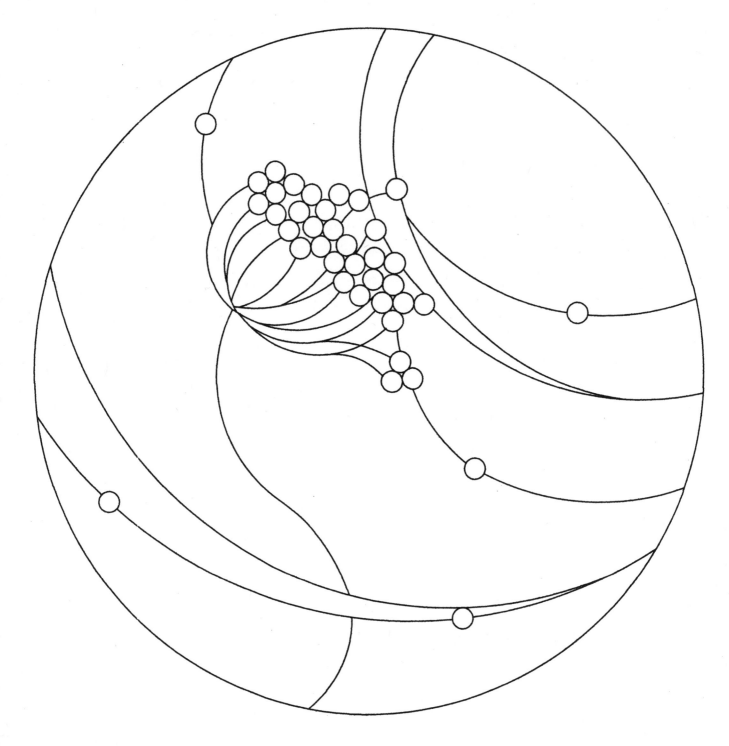

Flora Bubbles I

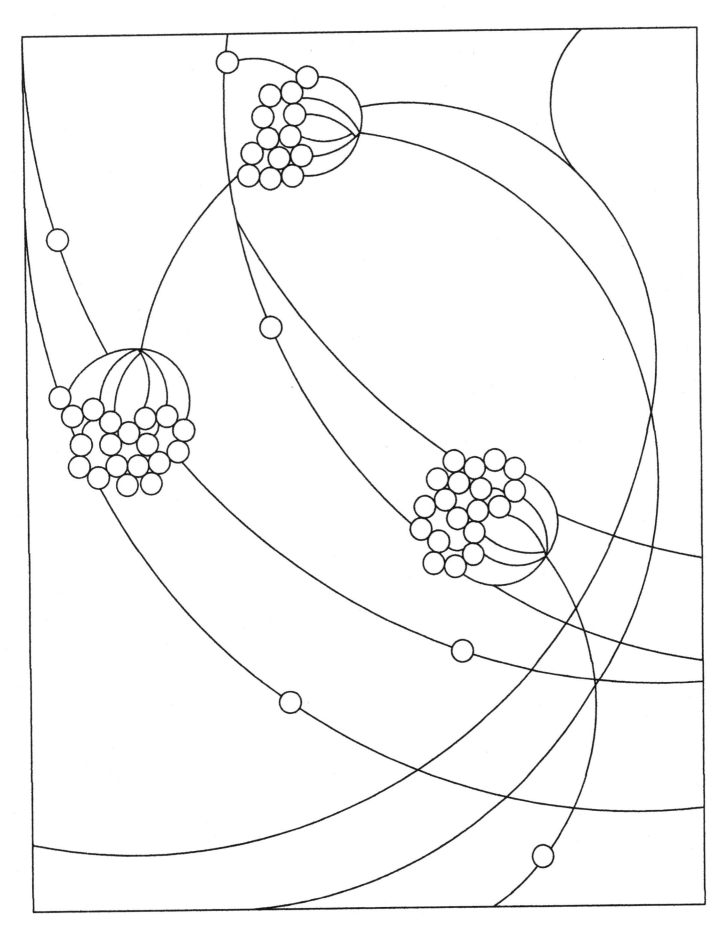

Flora Bubbles II

Lilies of the Water

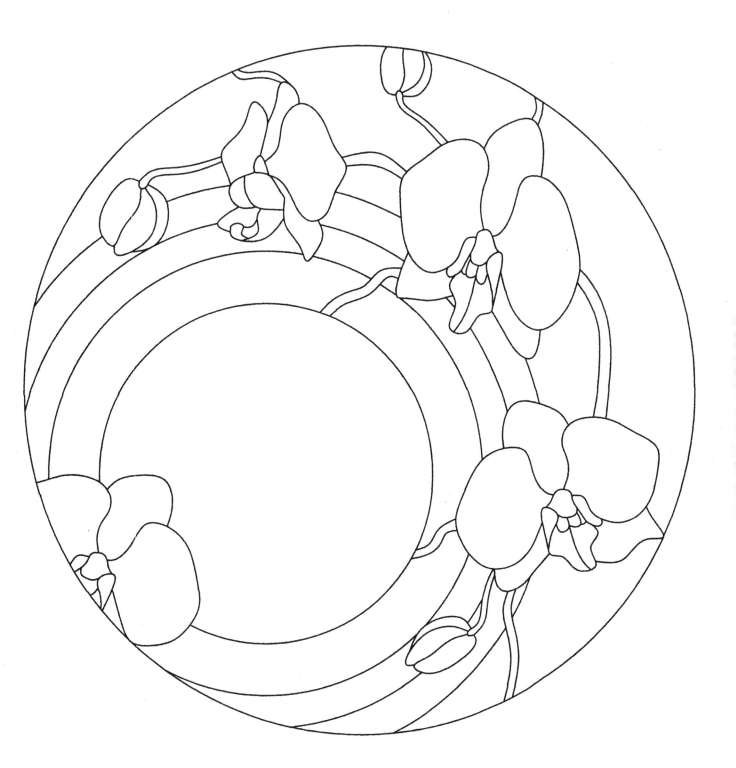

Lavender Butterfly

Cone Flower Cubes

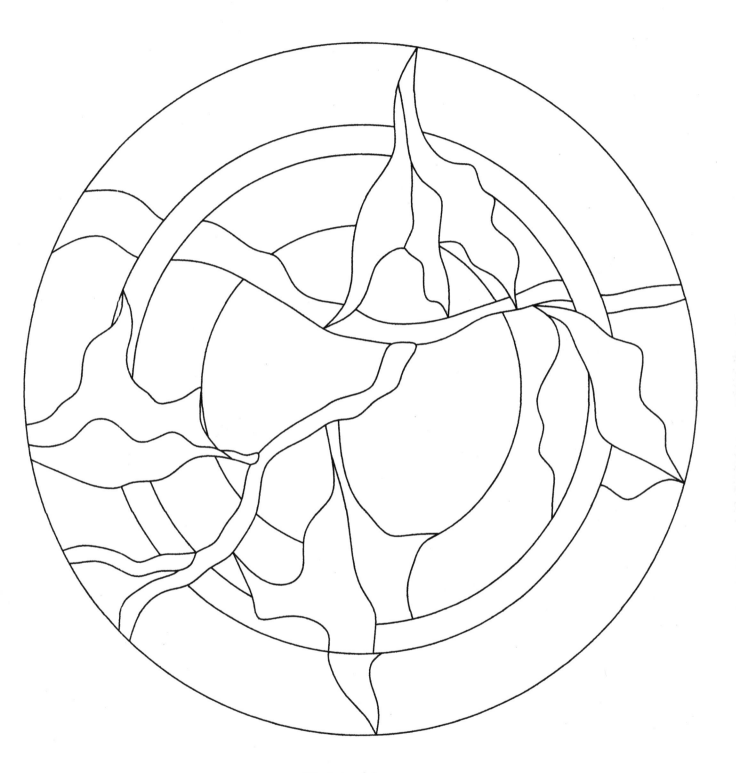

Twisted Leaves

Tree of Life

Pop Art Trees

Pineapple Punch

Modern Victorian

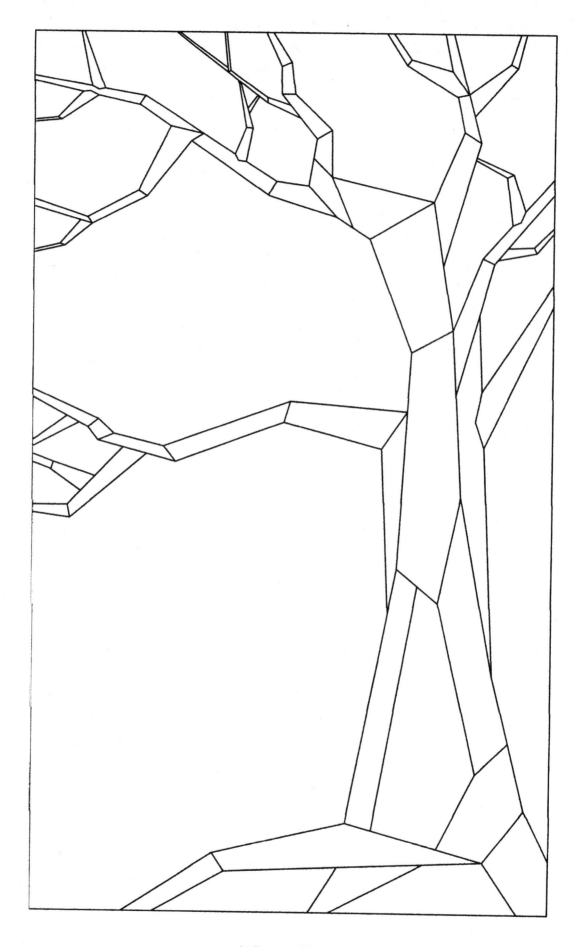

Winter Tree

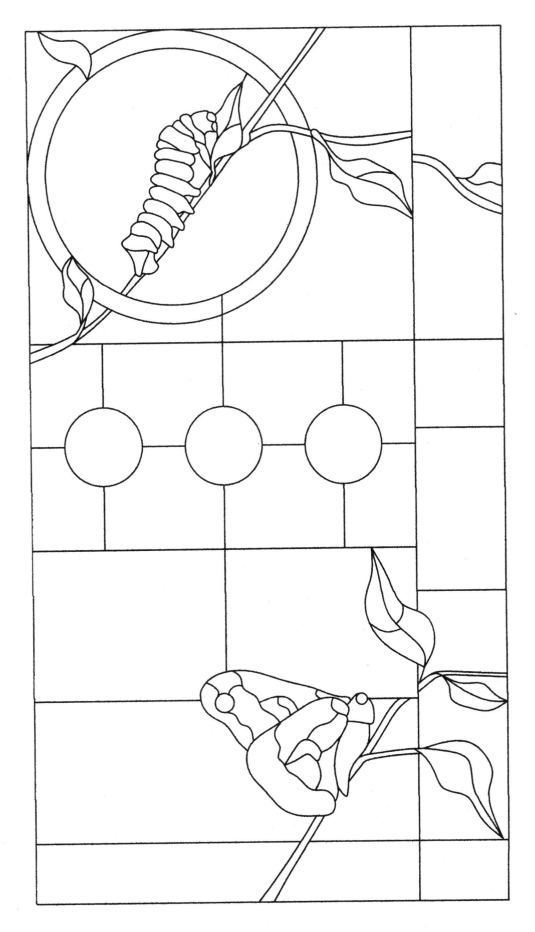

A Moth's Life

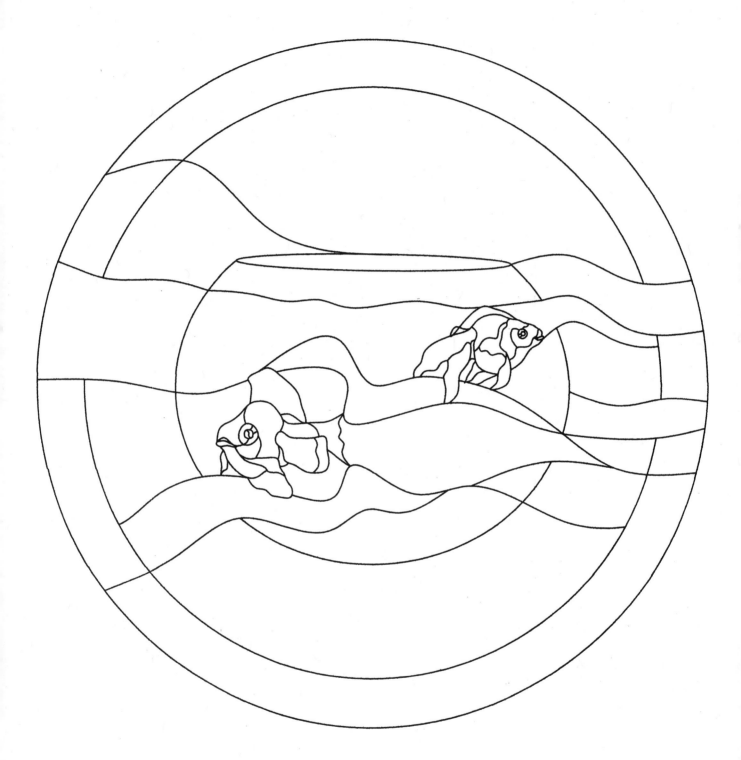

Life in a Fish Bowl

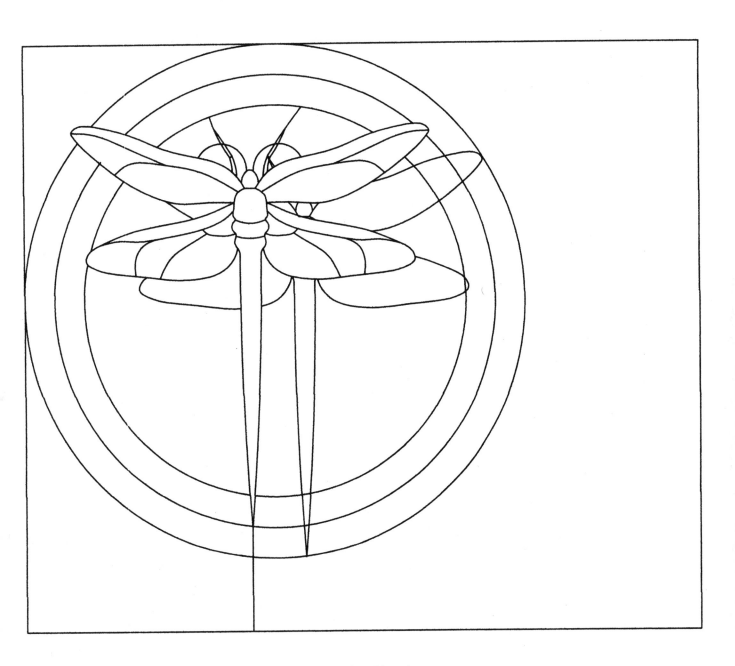

Dragonfly Shadows

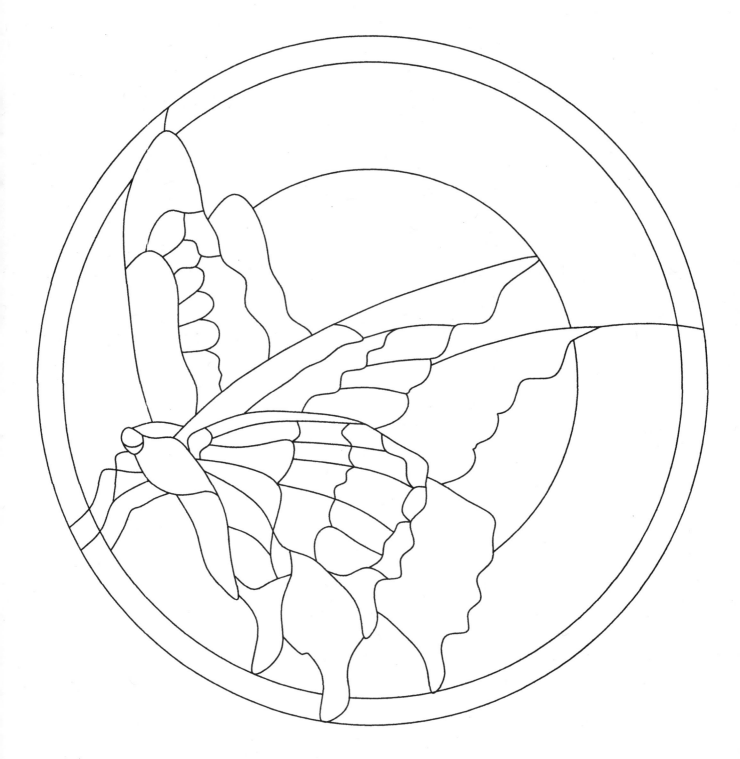

Butterfly Shadows

Deep Sea Dancer I

Deep Sea Dancer II

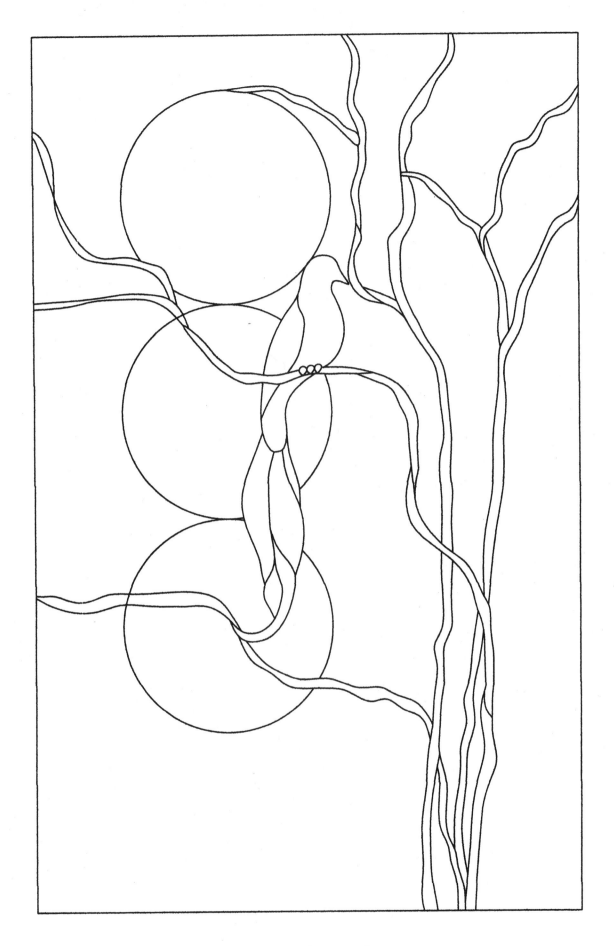

Moonlight Perch

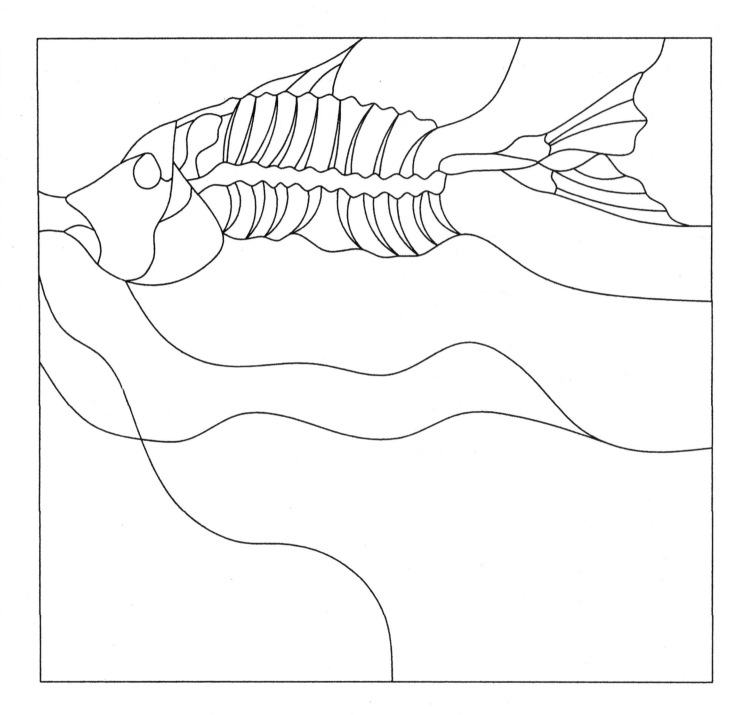

Fish Bones I

Fish Bones II

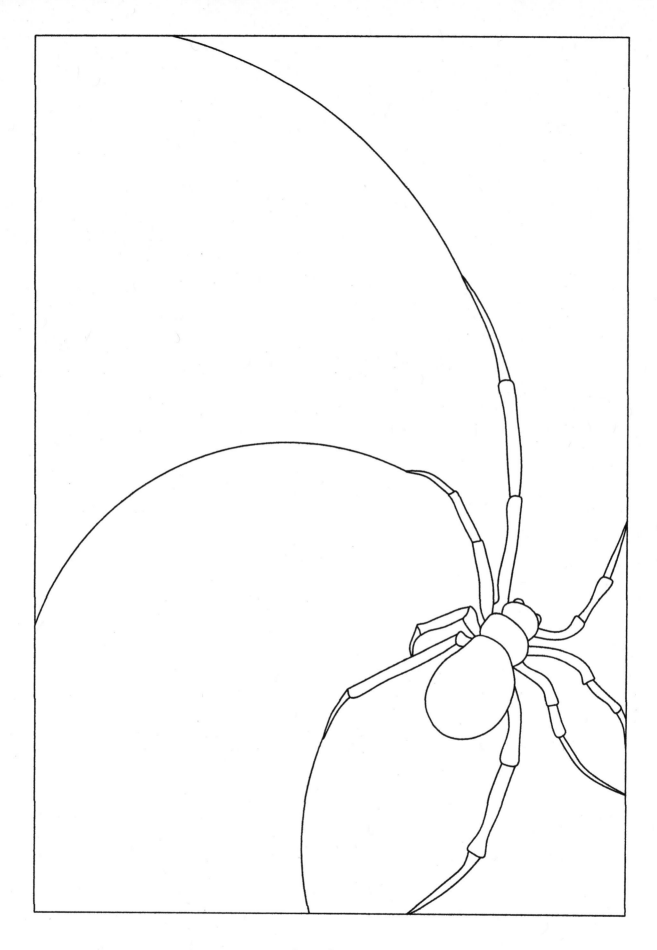

Itsy Bitsy

Ladybug Leaves

Monarch Magic

Beetle's Day

Mantis Leaves

p. 1. Peonies

p. 2. Loves Me, Loves Me Not

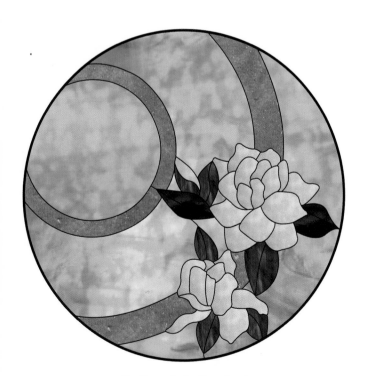

p. 3. Bonnie's Gardenia

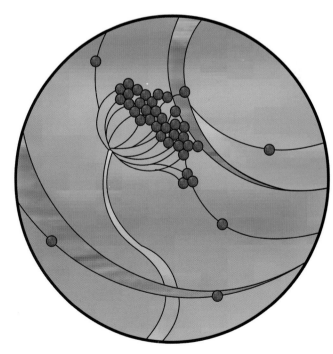

p. 4. Flora Bubbles I

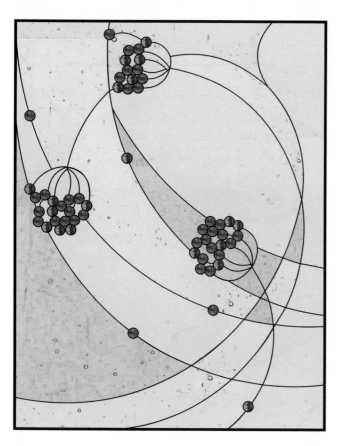

p. 5. Flora Bubbles II

p. 6. Lilies of the Water

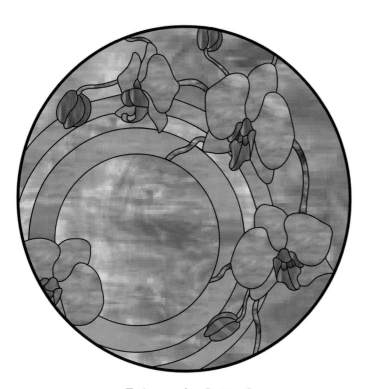

p. 7. Lavender Butterfly

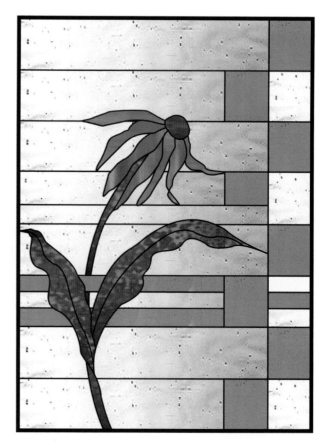

p. 8. Cone Flower Cubes

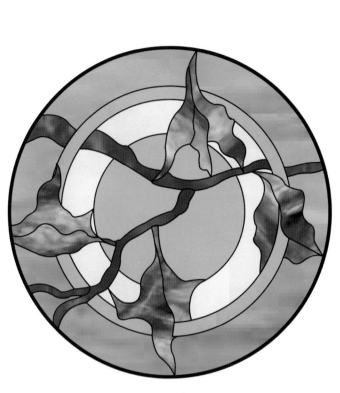

p. 9. Twisted Leaves

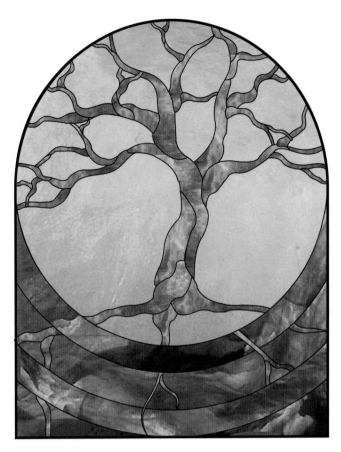

p. 10. Tree of Life

p. 11. Pop Art Trees

p. 12. Pineapple Punch

p. 13. Modern Victorian

p. 14. Winter Tree

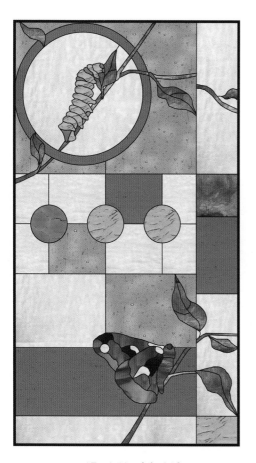

p. 15. A Moth's Life

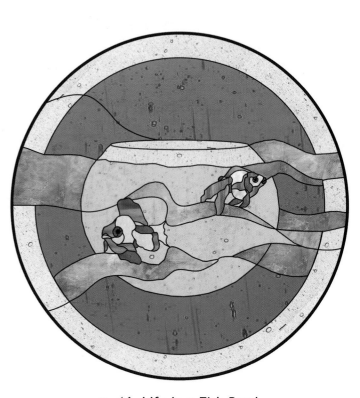

p. 16. Life in a Fish Bowl

p. 17. Dragonfly Shadows

p. 18. Butterfly Shadows

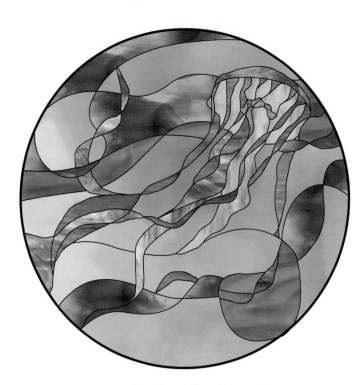

p. 19. Deep Sea Dancer I

p. 20. Deep Sea Dancer II

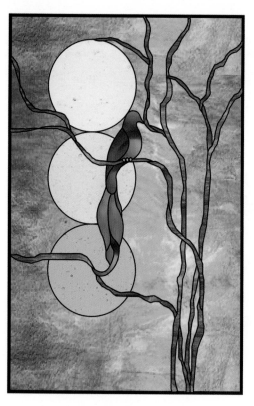

p. 21. Moonlight Perch

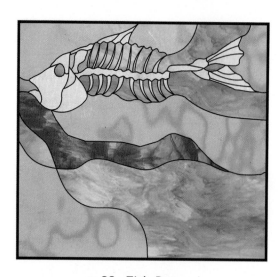

p. 22. Fish Bones I

p. 23. Fish Bones II

p. 24. Itsy Bitsy

p. 25. Ladybug Leaves

p. 26. Monarch Magic

p. 27. Beetle's Day

p. 28. Mantis Leaves

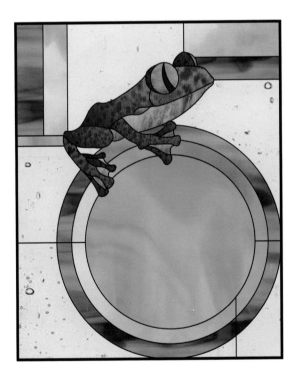

p. 29. Frog Bounce

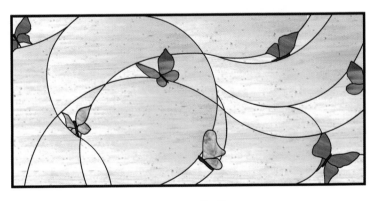

p. 30. Butterfly Breeze

p. 31. Winter Birds

p. 32. Dragonfly Tails

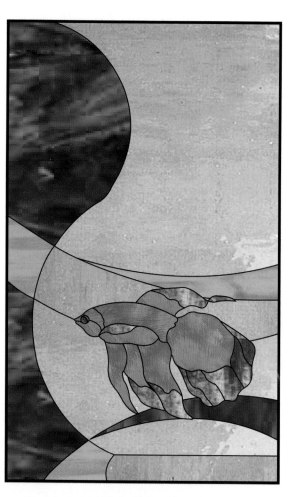

p. 33. Beta Fish

p. 34. Heavenly Hen

p. 35. Wake-Up Call

p. 36. Hummingbird's Point

p. 37. Steer Clear

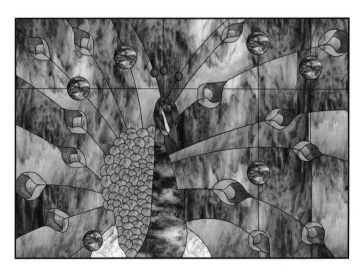

p. 38. Peacock Proud

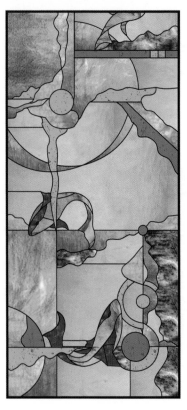

p. 39. Cosmic Koi

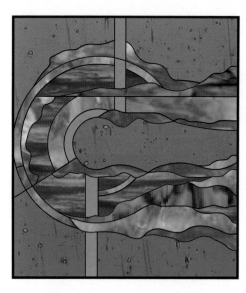

p. 40. Comet Closeup

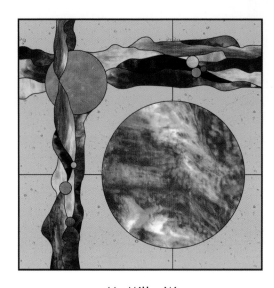

p. 41. Milky Way

p. 42. Storm Clouds

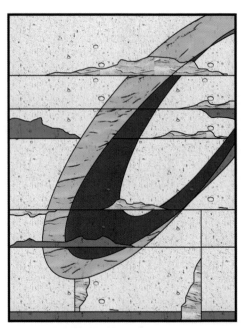

p. 43. Circles in the Sky I

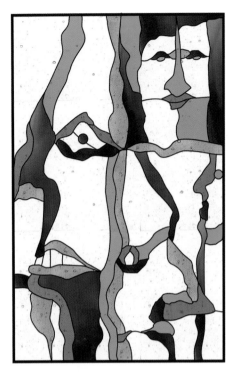

p. 44. Headcase I

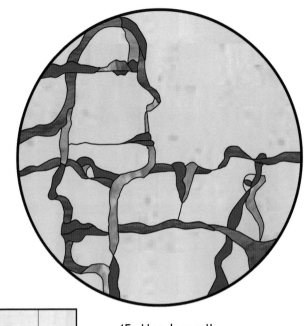

p. 45. Headcase II

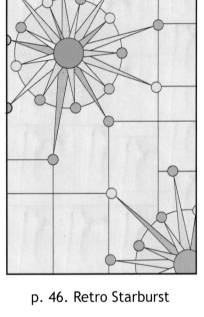

p. 46. Retro Starburst

p. 47. Tropically Retro

p. 48. Southwest Contempo I

p. 49. Southwest Contempo II

p. 50. Sun Burst

p. 51, *left*. Smoke I

p. 51, *right*. Smoke II

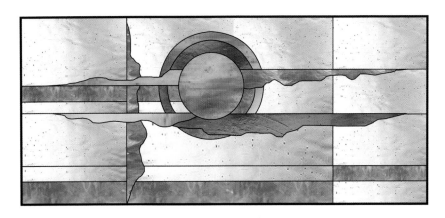

p. 52, *top*. Amber Skies

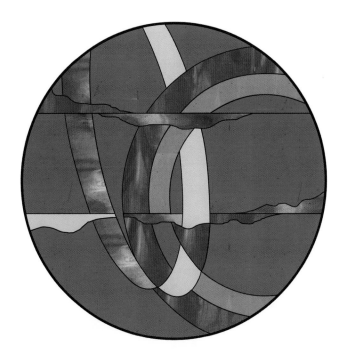

p. 52, *bottom*. Circles in the Sky II

p. 53, *top*. Night and Day

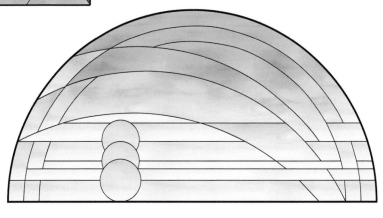

p. 53, *bottom*. Moon Rising

p. 54, *top*. Bonsai Sunset

p. 54, *bottom*. Morning Flight

p. 55, *top*. Water Drops

p. 55, *bottom*. Vector Round

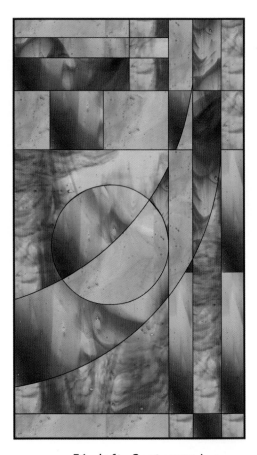

p. 56, *left*. Contempo I

p. 56, *right*. Contempo II

p. 57, *left*. Contempo III

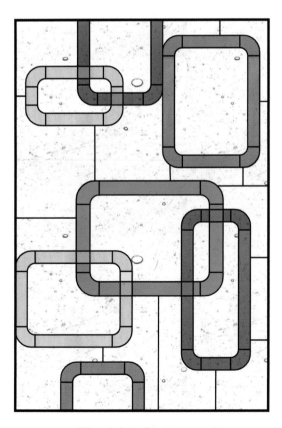

p. 57, *right*. Contempo IV

p. 58, *left*.
Woven Ribbons I

p. 58, *right*.
Woven Ribbons II

p. 59, *left*. Star Overlays

p. 59, *right*. Circles

p. 60, *left*. Pop Art Daisy

p. 60, *right*. Pop Art Leaves

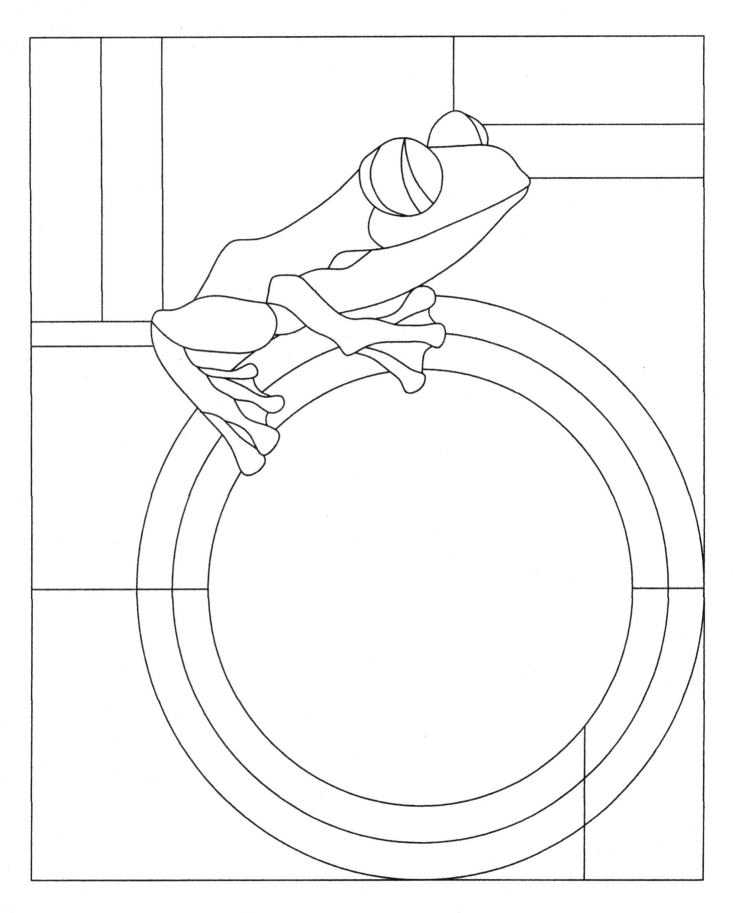

Frog Bounce

Butterfly Breeze

Winter Birds

Dragonfly Tails

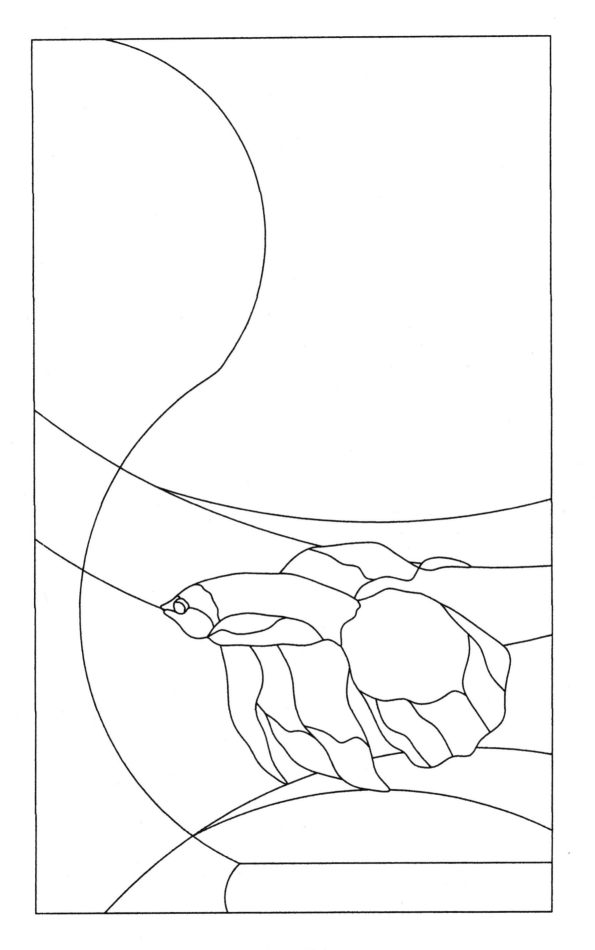

Beta Fish

Heavenly Hen

Wake-Up Call

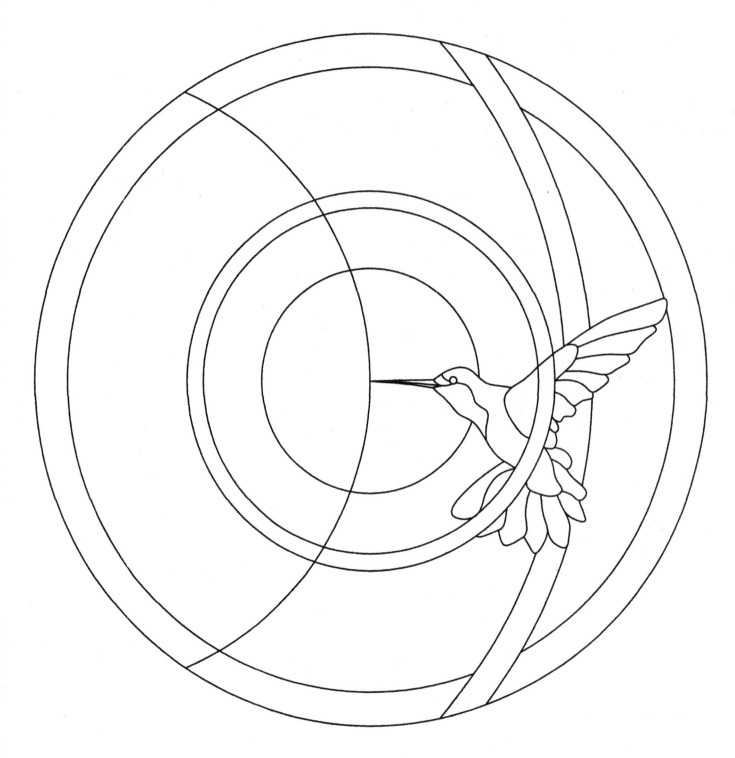

Hummingbird's Point

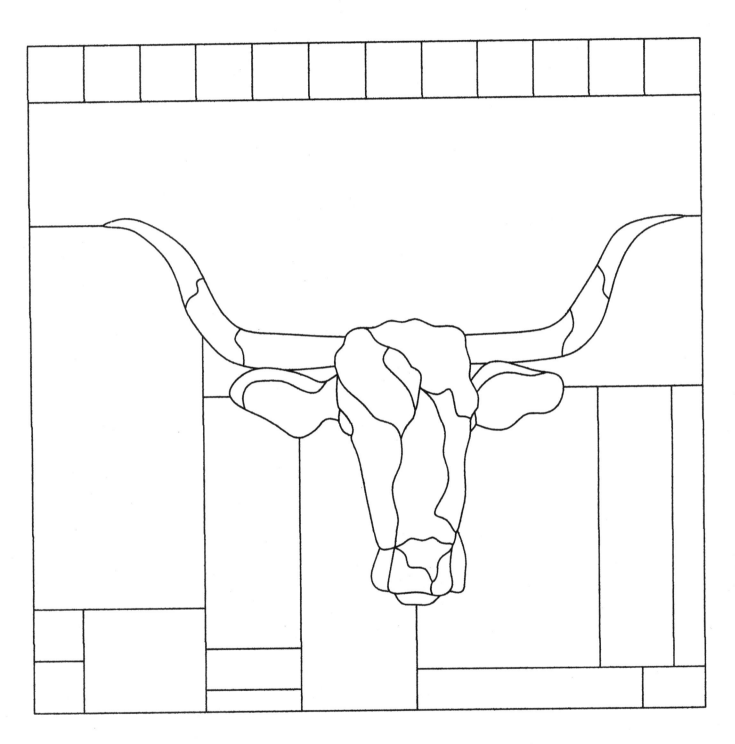

Steer Clear

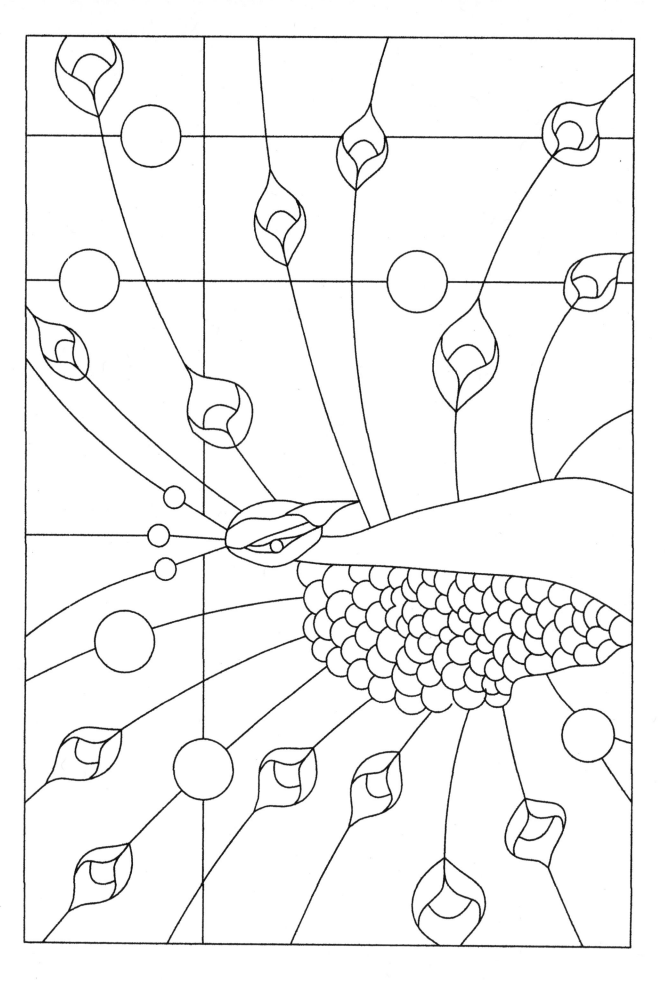

Peacock Proud

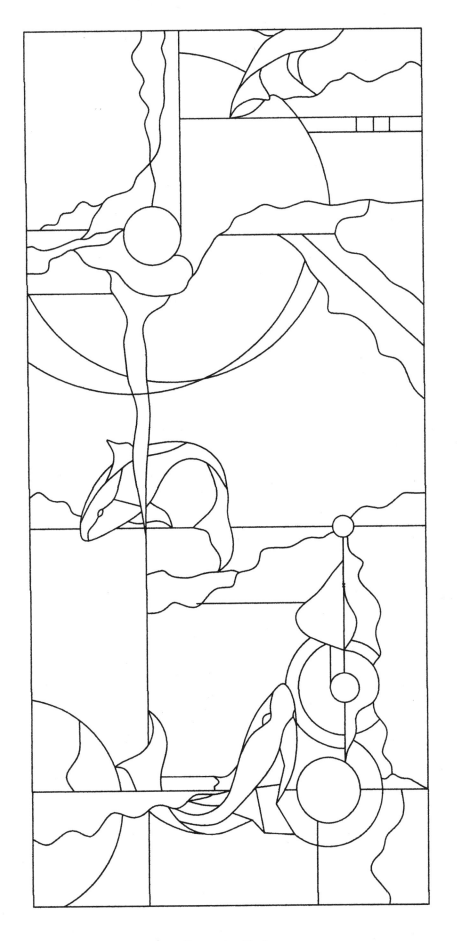

Cosmic Koi

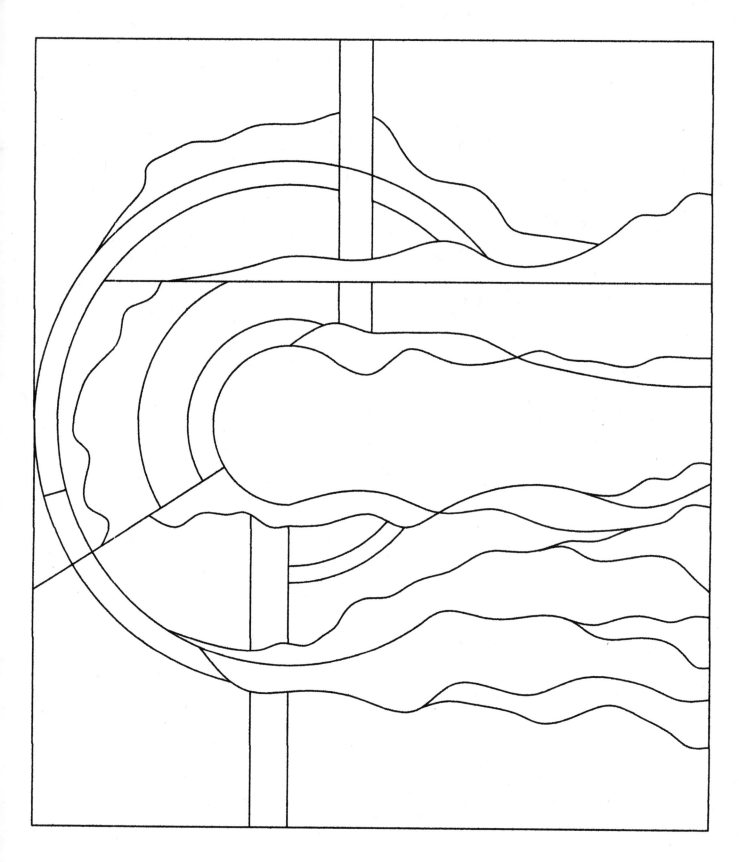

Comet Closeup

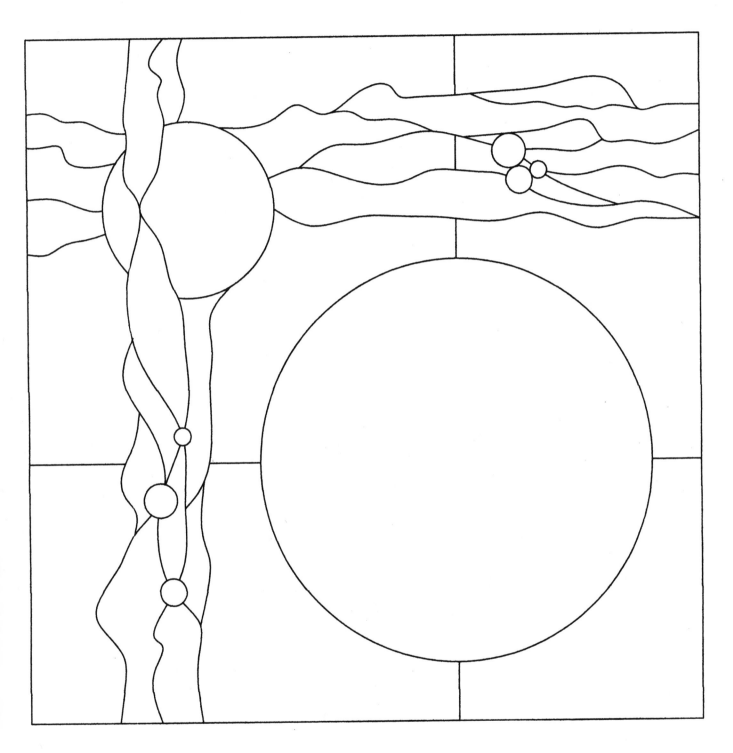

Milky Way

Storm Clouds

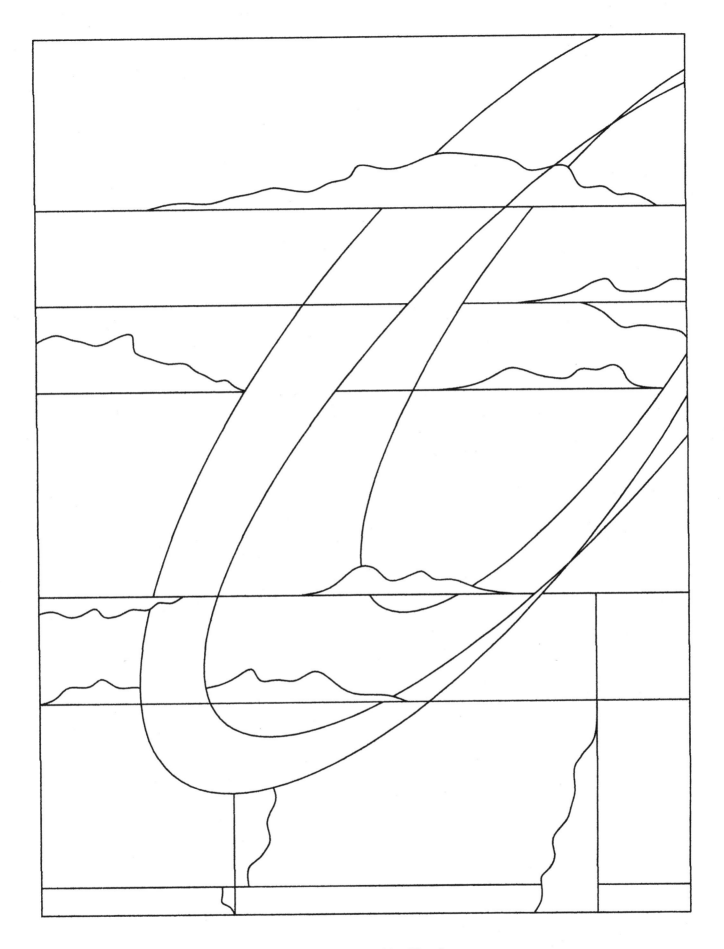

Circles in the Sky I

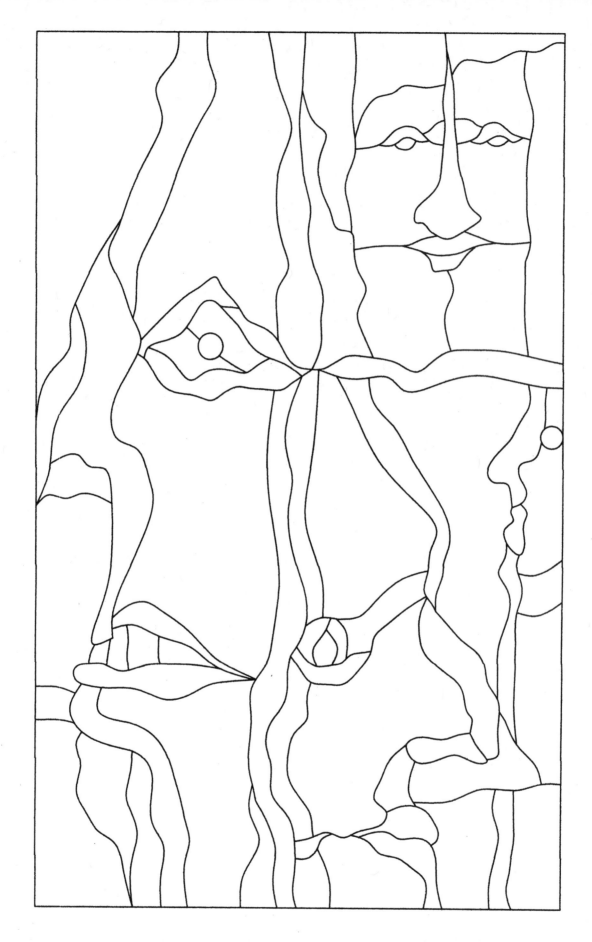

Headcase I

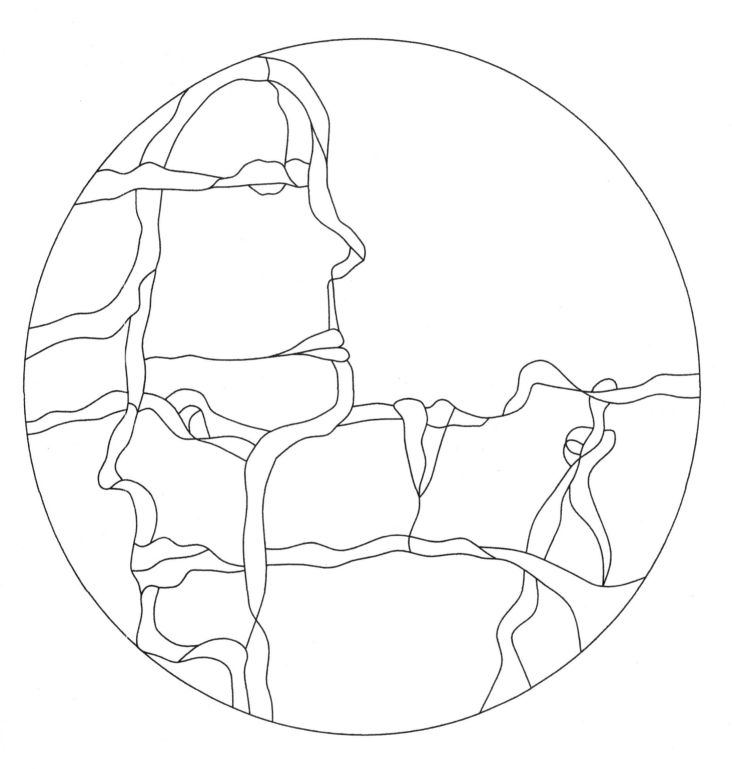

Headcase II

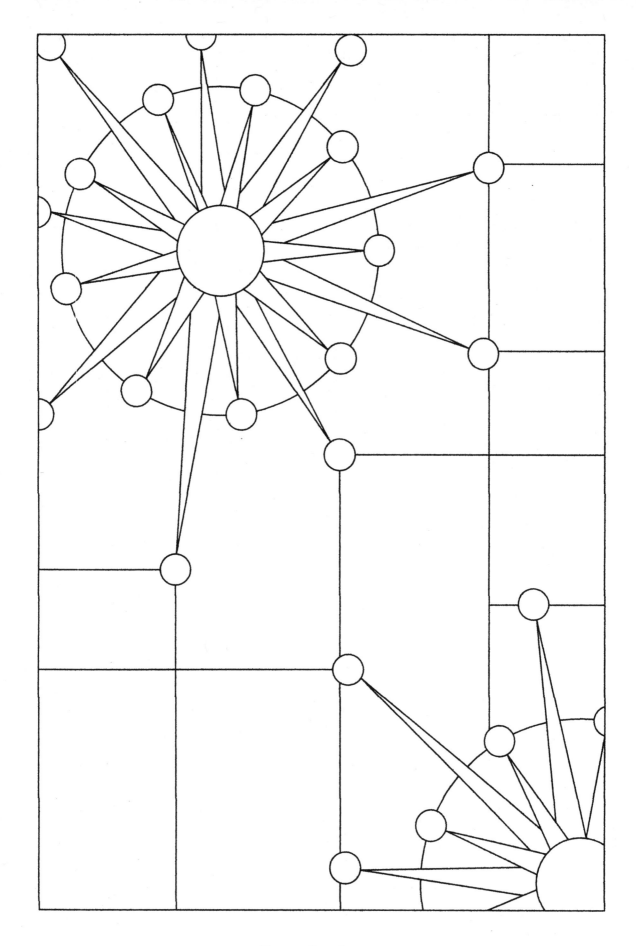

Retro Starburst

Tropically Retro

Southwest Contempo I

Southwest Contempo II

Sun Burst

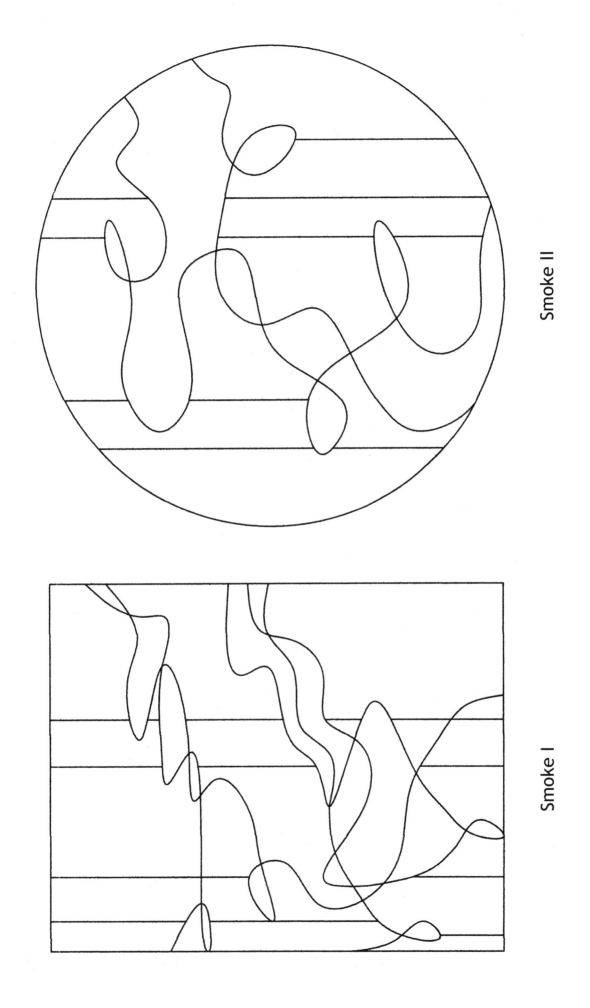

Smoke II

Smoke I

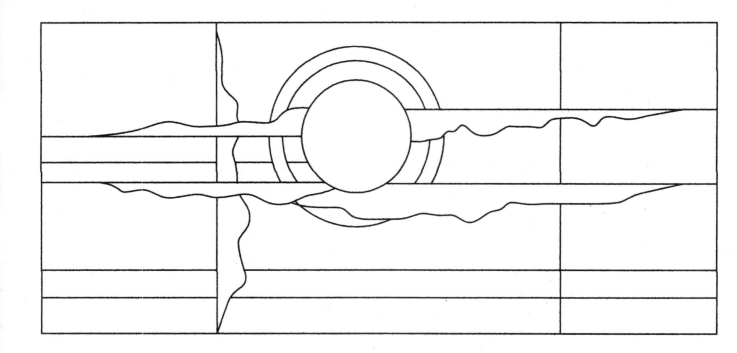

Amber Skies

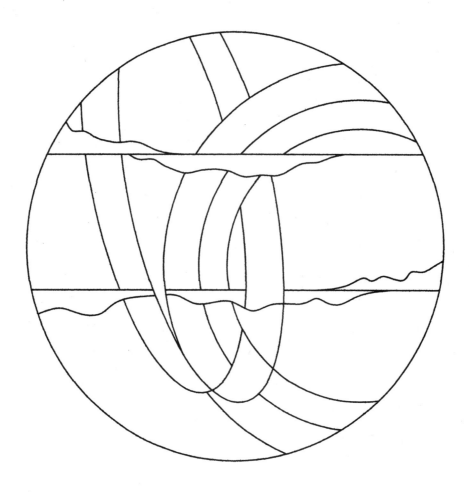

Circles in the Sky II

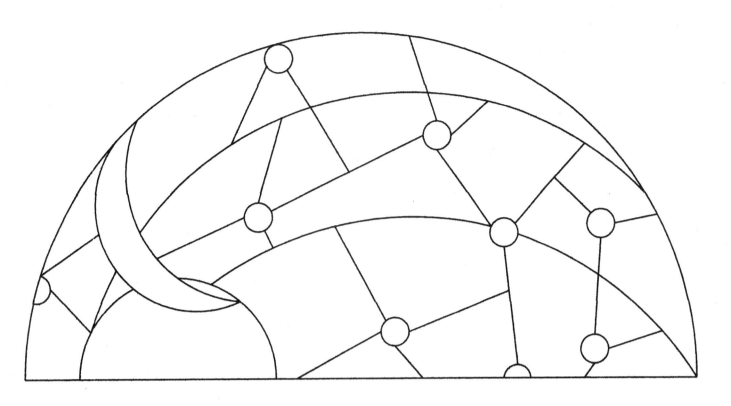

Night and Day

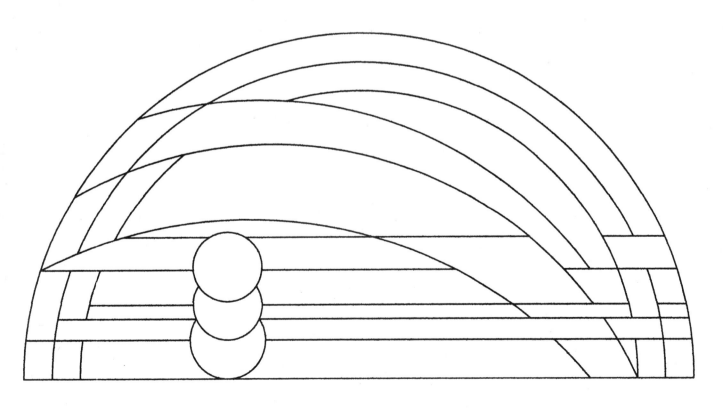

Moon Rising

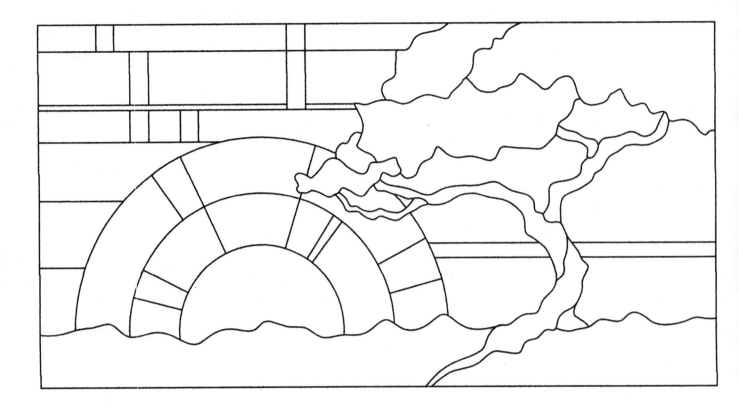

Bonsai Sunset

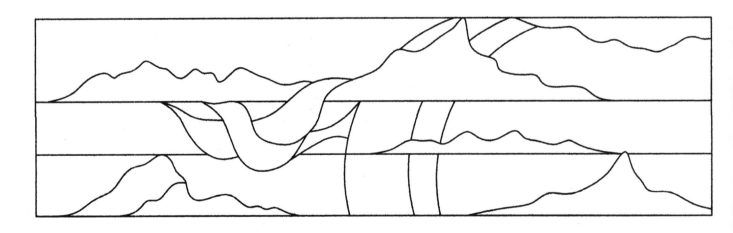

Morning Flight

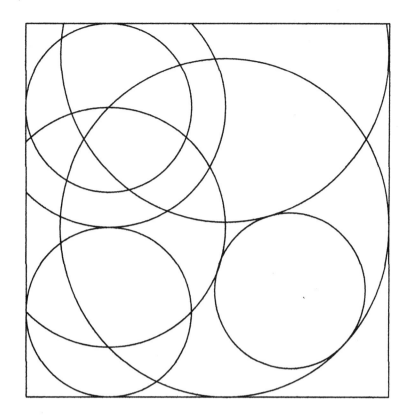

Water Drops

Vector Round

Contempo II

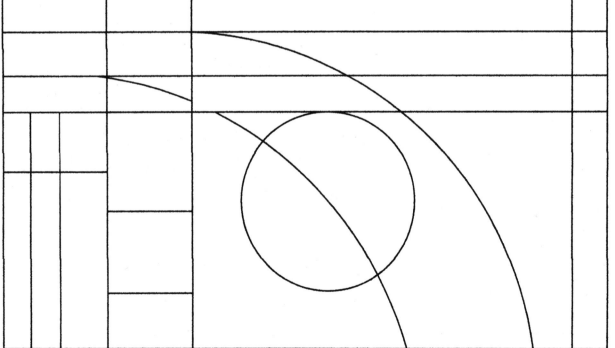

Contempo I

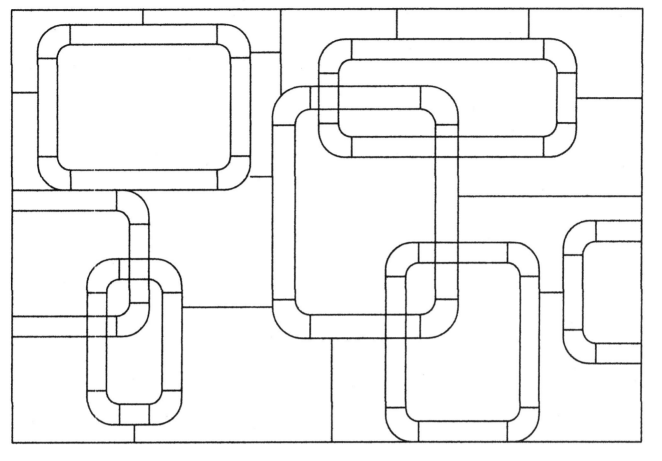

Contempo IV

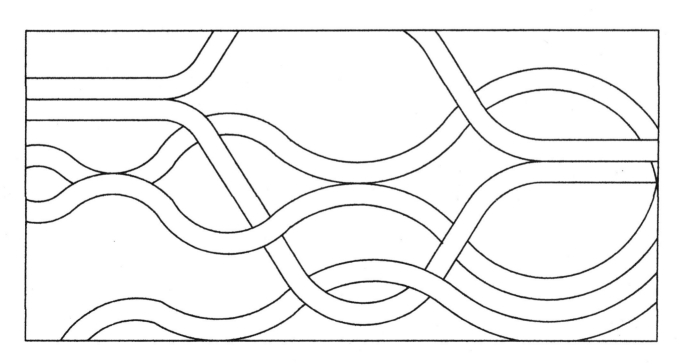

Contempo III

57

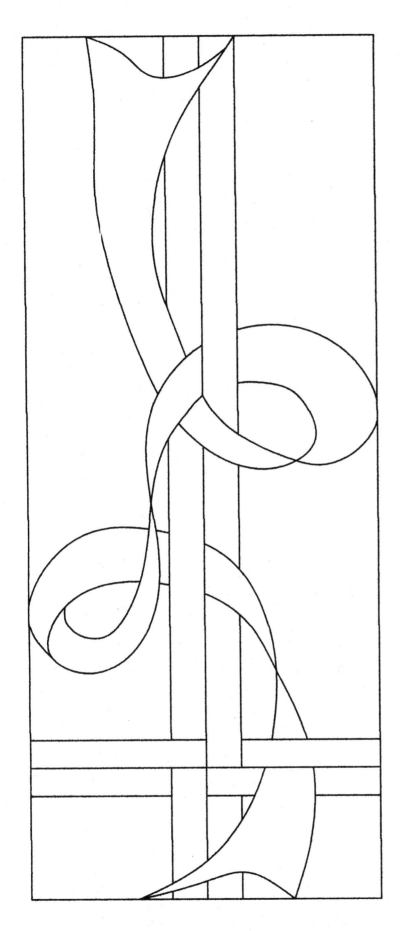

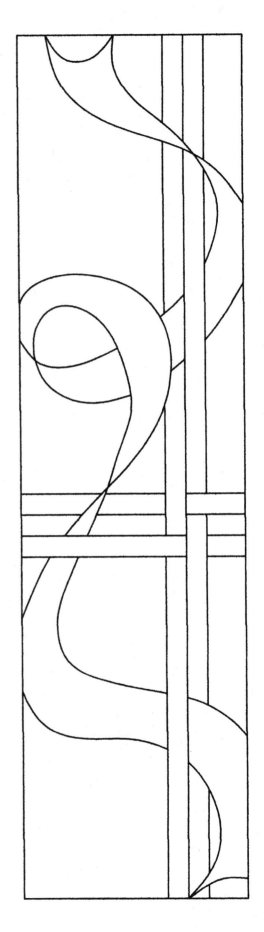

Woven Ribbons I

Woven Ribbons II

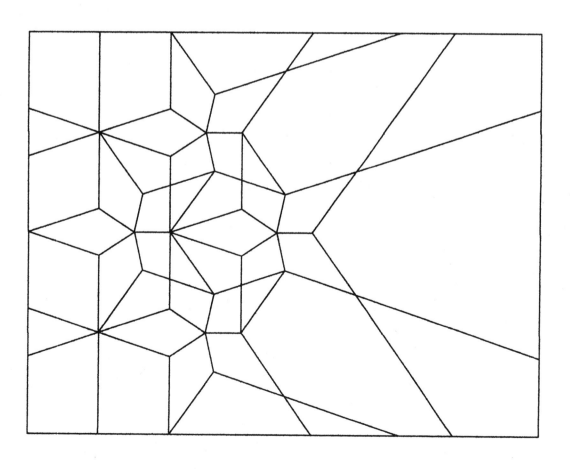

Circles

Star Overlays

59

Pop Art Leaves

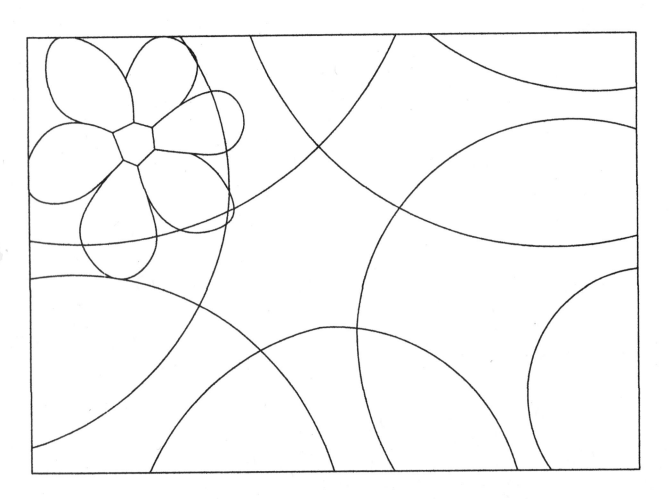

Pop Art Daisy

60